THE CRAFT KINGDOM

DIY and Crafts Projects

This book is dedicated to my mother, Hagit Maor, the most courageous and powerful woman I have ever known. In your life you were devoted to crafting in many ways, your creations touched so many people. In your last days you took care of yourself by crafting, that was a healthy comfort for you. Your admiration of my interests and your smile when you saw something new I created, gave me the strength and inspiration to bring this book to life. Thank you dear mom for teaching me to create from everything and for everyone. This book is dedicated to you.

Author: Eli Maor
Contact: maoreli@gmail.com
Graphic Design: Elad Maor, Eli Maor
Photography: Eytan Arditi, Eli Maor, Istock, Depositphotos
Published by AAHR Maor Offset, Ltd operated by Griddlers.net

Social Media
YouTube: http://bit.ly/CraftKingdomYoutube
Facebook: http://bit.ly/CraftKingdomFacebook
Instagram: http://bit.ly/CraftKingdomIG

Copyright © All Rights Reserved to AAHR Offset Maor Ltd.
1st Edition Printed: 2017
Printed in the USA

ISBN: 978-9657679463

What is crafting to me?
Ever since I was a child, I remember organizing my room and creating its aesthetic. When I was done organizing, I would put out the garbage and place unused things into a recycle pile. Jewelry, clothes, and tools were saved to be materials for future projects. Bracelets and pendants became keychains, clothes turned into patches, toilet paper rolls became wall decorations, and plates were broken into mosaics. These were only a few ways in which recyclables found new uses while I was an adolescent. Time has passed and today you just pay a visit to the nearest craft store and purchase anything you need, right? The fact is that you don't really need to use anything new. There is beauty in appreciating used items and seeing everything, old and new alike, as a legit craft material.
I have been asked numerous times, "Where did you get this?" When I answered, "I made it", I saw surprised expressions on people's faces. When we create something ourselves it is always a unique, singular, and original object that cannot be found in any store.
In the world of crafting there is a lot of freedom - freedom to create, to make art, to embellish. This is the time to break the rules and challenge the meaning of things around us while we create things with new artistic value. With that being said, It does not really matter what your art or craft looks like, as long as you created it.

Background
My name is Eli Maor.
I was raised in a home that breathed art and content. I absorbed creativity with my entire essence.
During my youth, I spent hours at my parent's publishing house - inhaling the color fumes from the printing machines, copying and cutting fonts on old light tables.
The publishing house was the first workshop I was exposed to.
Over the years, the passion for learning burned within me and I finished my B.A. in Media and business management, and later on started my interior design studies.
The media side exposed me to photography and editing.
The management side gave me the tools to manage a business.
In order to finance my college studies, I worked at art sales booths and sold handmade craft I created – jewelry, wreaths, hair accessories and anything that looked beautiful to me that could make any person or space happier, colorful and creative.
Along the way, I created hundreds of pixelart drawings in Griddlers.net. These drawings brought me recognition and a lot of love and appreciation. After my mom passed away I found comfort in creating and sharing my art. I started my YouTube channel that contains many of the ideas found in this book. The "Craft Kingdom" was born after years of working with any material I could get my hands on, workshops I taught, accumulating information about crafts and a lot of trial and error.
This book contains practical and creative information in order to inspire and motivate anyone to create and embellish everything they wish.

INTRO

So what do you need to get started?

Crafting and making art is very individual, the time you spend is completely yours. Even if you don't have access to all of the materials, you can be creative and experiment. Even if you prefer to use one type of material over another, or if you prefer glue over sewing, do it.
The main purpose is to enjoy it and create your vision at every moment. There is no need for any special skills for the projects in this book. However, those who sell artwork and wish to obtain the maximum results should stick to the projects and supplies as written. With that being said, there is no right or wrong way to craft and to make art, it comes down to having fun and express yourself.

Book Structure

This book contains more than 90 DIY, crafts and art projects. Under each category, you will find the required supplies for each project and a tutorial. At the end of the book, you will find templates that will help you trace shapes and silhouettes for the projects.

Projects that involve the use of hot glue guns, fire, scissors, knives or any tool that can be dangerous must be supervised by an adult.

TOC

Colors 8-20

Nature Craft 21-32

Stamps 33-35

Washi Tape 36-40

Soap Making 41-48

Candle Making 49-51

Recycling Art 52-59

Repurposing 60-66

Accessories 67-79

Fabric and Textile 80-86

Buttons 87-90

Paper 91-97

Paper Napkin 98-100

Templates 101-112

THINGS TO GET STARTED WITH

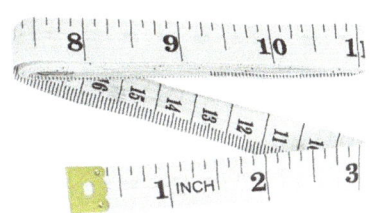

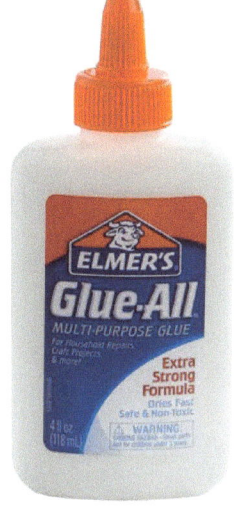

COLORS

Modern digital artwork can be created in any color you wish in less than a second, but mixing the colors by ourselves is something completely different. We may think that colors are predetermined, and what you see is what you get. However, by mixing blue, red and yellow, the three primary colors, we can create a million additional colors we never imagined could be contained. The color possibilities are infinite and this is what makes the painting process so enriching and creative. Keep in mind that colors are not just colors but an opportunity to create new shades, textures, shadows and a personal expression.

CREATING COLORS

- Black = Red, Blue, Yellow
- Grey = Black, White
- Brown = Red, Green
- Light Brown = Green, Orange
- Nude = Brown, Yellow
- Green = Blue, Yellow (more Yellow)
- Dark Green = Blue, Green
- Mint Green = Blue, Green, Yellow, White
- Purple = Red, Blue (more Red)
- Lilac Purple = Red, Blue, White
- Pink = Red, White
- Orange = Red, Yellow (more Yellow)
- Peach = Red, Yellow, White
- Turquoise = Blue, White, Green, Yellow (more White)

CREATING SHADES

If colors are diluted in water or white paint, they will fade and create new shades.
The world of shades gives dimension to anything you decide to paint.

FREEHAND PAINTING

PROJECT

Abstract painting is a form of pure art expressing itself through colors, shapes, textures and composition. The Abstract in a sense proves that we can all be artists, so grab a canvas, paints, and a dash of inspiration and start to express yourself.

OMBRE PAINTING

SUPPLIES

Canvas / Object
Paints
White Color
Painting Brush

PROJECT

Estimate how much paint you will need based on the size of the object you wish to paint.
Mix the paint with white paint, about a quarter of the amount, and mix the colors until you get a lighter shade of color.
You will be creating several tints of the same color. Start with your original color. This will be the first and darkest shade you will be using.
After you finish painting with that shade add enough white to the paint to make it a little lighter tint. This is your second color that you use to paint.
After painting with that color add more white, then paint. Finally add more white and paint again creating the ombré technique.

SPONGE PAINTING TEXTURE

SUPPLIES

Canvas / Object
Paints
Sponge

PROJECT

Drip the colors you choose onto a flat plate or palette.
Dip the sponge lightly into the paint.
Gently dab the sponge onto the object until it is completely painted and you have a texture you like.

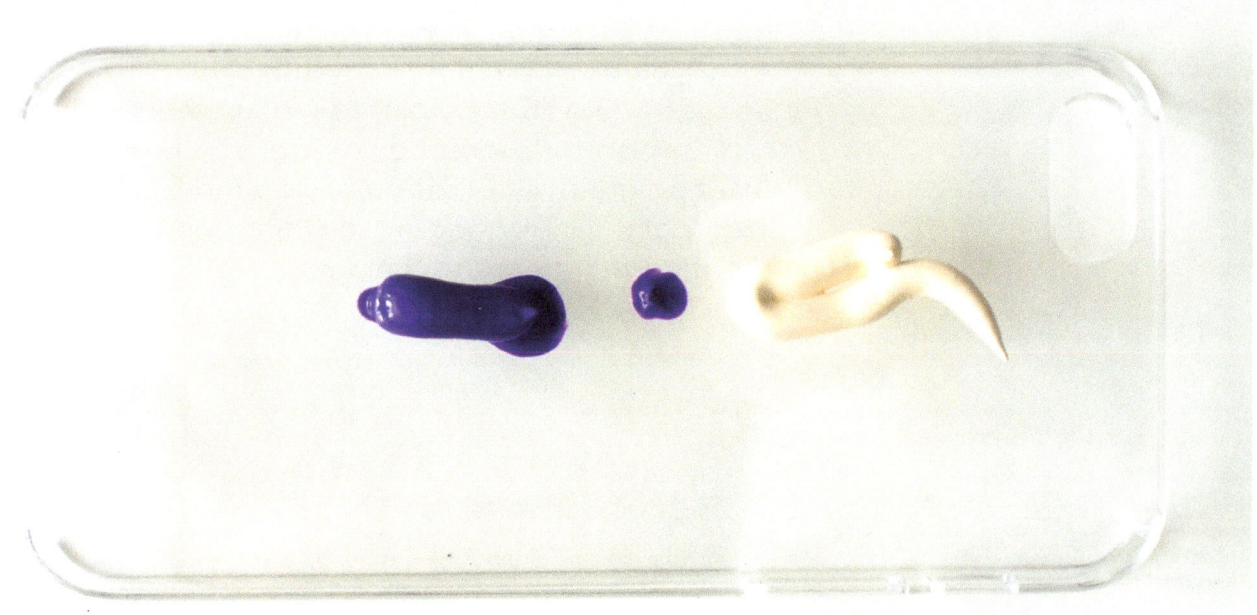

The Craft Kingdom

HOW TO CREATE TEXTURE

SUPPLIES

Canvas / Object
Small Roller
String / Yarn
Paints

PROJECT

Wind the string around the roller and tie it at the end. Dip the roller in the paint and roll it on your surface until you create your desired texture.

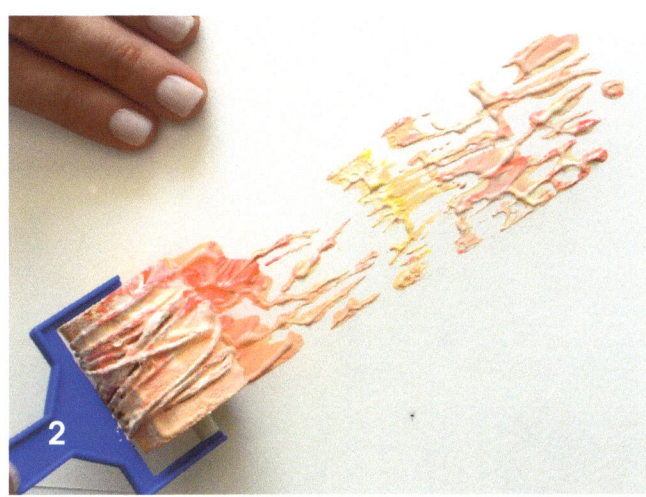

THE DISTRESSED LOOK

SUPPLIES

Canvas / Object
Colors
Paintbrush
Sandpaper

PROJECT

Paint the object and wait until the paint dries. After the paint dries gently sand off some of the paint using circular motions.

GEOMETRIC PAINTING

SUPPLIES

Canvas / Object
Colors
Paintbrush
Tape

PROJECT

Glue the tape on the canvas in different directions. Paint the canvas with the colors you selected and remove the tape carefully. Set the paint to dry.

NAIL POLISH PAINTING

SUPPLIES

Canvas / Object
Nail Polishes

PROJECT

Paint any object you choose using nail polish. Use acetone or nail polish remover to make corrections in your design.

NAIL POLISH MARBLEIZING

SUPPLIES

Mug / Cup
Nail Polishes
Container
Water

PROJECT

Pour water into a container that will be large enough to submerge you subject, and drip the nail polishes into the container as well. Hold the mug by its handle and dip it into the water. Set the mug to dry.

The Craft Kingdom — Want more Projects? Visit us on Youtube

HOT GLUE GUN PAINTING

SUPPLIES

Hot Glue Gun
Canvas / Object
Paints

PROJECT

Plug in the hot glue gun and allow it to heat up. Use the hot glue gun as a paintbrush and decorate as you wish. For a polished look, paint the object and allow it to dry.

POUR PAINTING

SUPPLIES
Vase / Glass Container
Paints

PROJECT
Clean the container of dust or dirt to ensure that the paint will stick.

Pour a small amount of paint into the vase and start tipping and turning until the paint covers the inside of the vase and set aside to dry.

STENCIL PAINTING

SUPPLIES

Canvas / Object
Spray Paint
Tape / Stencil

PROJECT

Use the tape to cover the area you do not wish to paint. If you choose to use a stencil, place it where you wish to decorate and affix it using the tape. Make sure you use the spray in an open space with fresh air. Shake the can from time to time. Spray short swipes across the painting. Be careful to keep the can moving so that it does not puddle on your surface. Continue until you get full coverage. Remove the tape or stencil gently, and set aside to dry.

HOW TO SKETCH

SUPPLIES

Regular / Tracing Paper
Regular and colored
Penciles
Printer

PROJECT

A quick visit to internet land will expose you to many illustration guides such as this.
If it is hard for you to copy images, you can always trace the object figure using a transparent paper.

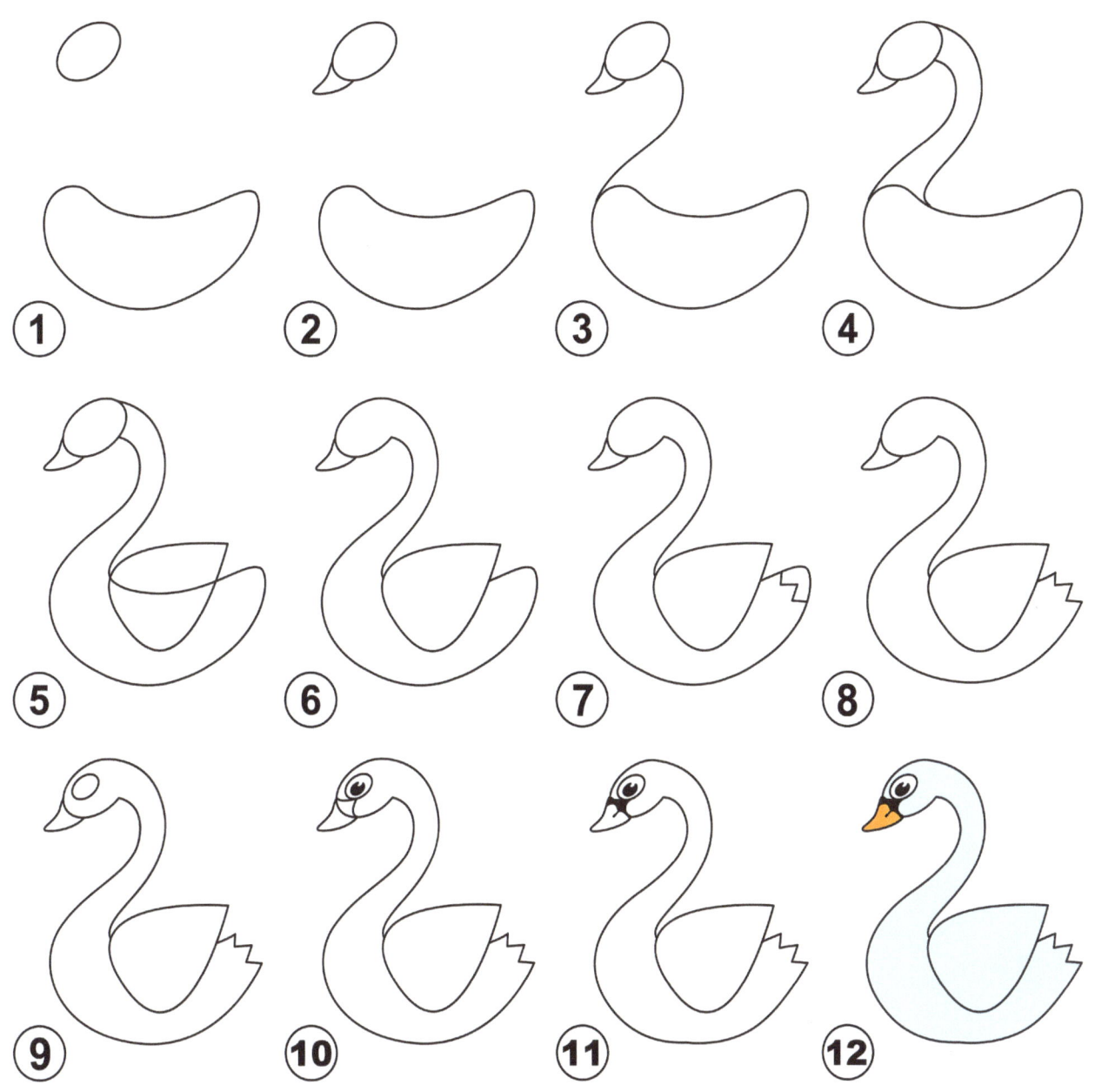

HOW TO PAINT ANYTHING

Paint can cover almost any object you can think of.
So, do not hesitate and bring new life to any object you love.

NATURE CRAFT

The variety of smells, sounds, textures, and colors provided by nature are sometimes unimaginiable.
Very often the hectic modern lifestyle makes us forget the natural wonders.
A short walk outside reveals a world with exciting raw materials - leaves, wood, branches, stones, flowers, sand, shells and more, all of these can be turned into art.
So before you rush off to the craft store, take a walk outside, you will be surprised to discover the amount of raw materials nature has to offer.

BRANCHES

Branches are an amazing raw material for indoor as well as outdoor decorating. You can paint and glue them easily.
Even in their clean and natural state, branches beautify any space and bring a bit of nature into our home.

FLOWERY BRANCHES

SUPPLIES

Branches
Artificial Flowers
Hot Glue Gun
Scissors

PROJECT

Clean the branches of dust or dirt. Cut the flower stems and glue the flowers on the branches.

GLITTERED BRANCHES

SUPPLIES

Branches
Glitter Glue /
Glitter Nail Polish
Paintbrush

PROJECT

Clean the branches of dust or dirt and apply a layer of glitter glue or glitter nail polish. Wait for the branch to dry and repeat until the branch is fully covered.

DECORATING WITH BRANCHES

SUPPLIES
Template (Page 102-104)
Branches
Clippers
Hot Glue Gun
Tape
A4 Cardboard
Scissors

PROJECT
Cut out the template carfully (Page 102-104) and clean the branches of dust or dirt. Cut the branches into equal pieces following the templates. If the branches have sharp edges smooth them using sandpaper or a nail file. Secure the template using the tape and glue the branches following the template. Cut around the template and glue the object in the center of the cardboard and set to dry.

The Craft Kingdom — Want more Projects? Visit us on Youtube

BRANCHED OBJECTS

SUPPLIES

Glass
Branches
Clippers
Hot Glue Gun

PROJECT

Clean the branches of dust or dirt and cut them into equal pieces to match the height of the glass. If the branches have sharp edges smooth them using sandpaper or a nail file. Glue the branches vertically on the glass using a hot glue gun, and set to dry.

The Craft Kingdom

LEAVES
Use leaves and twigs to decorate gifts for your loved ones

PAINTED LEAVES

SUPPLIES
Leaves
Spray Paint

PROJECT
Select leaves of different sizes and textures with which you want do decorate. Clean the leaves of dust. Paint the leaves, and make sure you coat the entire leaf surface. Wait for them to dry and use them as decorations.

LEAFY PLACE CARDS

SUPPLIES
Leaves
Scissors
Squared Papers
Glue

PROJECT
Pick fresh or painted leaves, clean them of dust and cut their stems. Fold the paper in half to create a rectangle that can stand of the front. Glue the leaves in the center of the folded card and leave room for your guests' names.

SHELLS AND CONCHES

Shells and conches are exciting sea treasures.
They come in a variety of textures, colors and sizes and last for years.
They can be painted, glued and decorated on almost anything.

SHELL FRAMES

SUPPLIES

Frame
Shells / Conches
Hot Glue Gun

PROJECT

Clean the frame of dust, and glue the shells or conches to the frame. Decorate as you wish and set to dry.

WOOD

PROJECT 1
Hang naked wood branches using hemp or rope.

PROJECT 2
Hang wood frame on a chalkboard or painted wall.

PROJECT 3
Place wooden boxes on top of each other to make shelves.

PROJECT 4
Tree trunks can warm any space, used as a chair or as a table.

PEBBLE MAGNETS

SUPPLIES
Flat Pebbles
Magnets
Hot Glue Gun

PROJECT
Place the pebble on its flat side, and glue the magnet to the center of the pebble. After the glue is dry, place the pebbles on the refrigerator or any magnetic surface.

DECORATED STONES

PROJECT
Decorating stones is a fun craft because stones have enough surface to paint, write or draw on.
Use your imagination and look at stones as canvases.

STAMPS

One of the most enjoyable ways to decorate and embellish is by stamping. So what about creating them yourself using unusual objects?

The Craft Kingdom

FLOWER STAMP FROM CELERY

SUPPLIES

Celery Root
Knife
Paint
Paper / Canvas / Object

PROJECT

Cut the celery near its root. Clean it of dirt using a dry towel.
Dip the celery in paint and stamp.

SPONGE STAMP

SUPPLIES

Sponge / Dish Sponge
Pen
X-Acto Knife
Paint
Paper / Canvas / Object

PROJECT

Draw any shape you wish in the center of the sponge. Cut it out and remove any sponge residues. Dip the sponge into the paint and stamp.

ERASER STAMP

SUPPLIES

Eraser
Pen
X-Acto Knife
Paint
Paper / Canvas / Object

PROJECT

Draw any shape you wish in the center of the eraser, cut it out and remove any leftovers. Dip the eraser in paint and stamp. You can repeat the same process on top of a pencil eraser to create a smaller stamp.

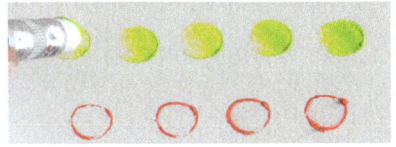

CORK STAMP

SUPPLIES

Cork
Pen
X-Acto Knife
Paint
Paper / Canvas / Object

PROJECT

Draw any shape you wish in the center of the cork and cut it out. Remove any cork leftovers, dip it in paint and stamp.

The Craft Kingdom — Want more Projects? Visit us on Youtube

WASHI TAPE

The original Washi Tape is a Japanese tape made from rice paper. This feature allows it to be removed easily without leaving any adhesive residue. Washi Tape is a spectacular printed artwork for decorating papers, albums, furniture, glasses and more.
This chapter does not contain any tutorials, just creativity.
Choose the object you wish to decorate and play with your imagination using the washi tape.

ENVELOPES DECORATION

PAPER DECORATION

NOTEBOOK DECORATION

PENCILS DECORATION

FURNITURE DECORATION

CAKE FLAGS DECORATION

CANDLES DECORATION

BOTTLE DECORATION

GIFT WRAP DECORATION

SOAP MAKING

Industrial soap making is a process that usually takes place in a laboratory under strictly supervised temperatures and metrics condotions.
In this chapter, I will share two simple techniques, that can be done at your own home.
The first, is melting soap leftover bits of soap and pouring them into molds.
The second, is melting raw soap flakes, enriching them with oils, and pouring them into a mold.
This chapter will open up a magical world of scents, textures, and health benefits.
Prepare yourselves for an aromatic as well as creative activity.
Children under 14 must be accompanied by an adult.

SOAP MELTING METHODS

Double Boiler or Bain-Marie

A method borrowed from the world of fine cooking that uses two stacked pots to make a double boiler. For soap melting, we will use a pot and heat-resistant glass utensil. Do not use a plastic utensil or any unknown material. This method is used when direct fire will harm the quality of materials or burn them. Because soap is a very heat-sensitive material, it can easily decompose. Therefore, turn off the fire before the soap is completely liquefied. The boiling water will help the soap to fully melt.

Microwave

Melting soap in the microwave must be done using a heat-resistant glass utensil. Use 10 to 20 second coocking times, according to microwave strength.

SILICON MOLDS AND COOKIE CUTTERS

Kitchen stores offer a wide variety of silicon molds in countless designs that can be used for soap making as well.

If you do not have a silicon mold available, you can pour the soap into any heat resistance container. Once the soap dry, cut it into different shapes using a cookie cutter.

RECYCLING LEFTOVER BITS OF SOAP

SUPPLIES

Soap Leftovers
Heat Resistant Glass Utensil
Fire / Microwave
Mixing Tool
Silicon Mold /
Heat Resistant Container
Alcohol Spray

PROJECT

Put the soap leftovers into a heat-resistant glass utensil and melt them. If you are using a double pot turn the fire off before the soap completely liquefies and mix slowly to retain the soap's temperature and texture. Once the soap melts and is liquefied, pour it into a mold and wait patiently for it to dry. For a polished look, spray alcohol on the soap when it's liquid, to free air bubbles. Soap takes 12-24 hours to dry, depending on room temperature. If you don't have the patience, the process can be sped up by placing the soap in the freezer for 2-3 hours, depending on freezer strength. After the soap is completely dried, pull it gently from the mold.

PERSONALIZED SOAP

Melt and Pour soap making is an amazing technique because it allows you to personalize your ideal soap - from design and scent to medical benefits, by using recommend oils for your skin.

RECOMMENDED OILS FOR THE SKIN

Before you randomly mix oils into your soap, take a closer look and find out what is the best oil for your skin.

Lavender Oil – Recommended for treating injuries, scrapes, stings and burns. Mainly use for inflammation, redness, rashes, acne, psoriasis and restores skin tissues.

Oregano Oil – Cures skin and scalp infections, encourage hair growth, and cures bacterial and fungal infections.

Grapefruit Oil – Burns fatty tissue, disinfects and absorbs liquids. Recommend for cellulite and stretch marks.

Rose Hip Oil – Contains a lot of essential fatty acids. Helps treat wrinkles, scars and cuts.

Bergamot Oil – Recommended for treating psoriasis and infections. Anti-inflammatory.

Carrot Oil – Accelerates the healing of wounds and burns and nourishes dry and scarred skin.

Geranium Oil – Treats scarred skin, acne, capillaries, and fungus. Recommended for stings.

Myrtle Oil – Disinfects oily acne skin and help sore muscles.

Tea Tree Oil – Prevents skin itchiness. Recommended for inflammations, burns and fungus.

Wheat Sprout Oil – Contains a high amount of antioxidants, mainly vitamin E that is responsible for preserving, restoring and maintaining skin cells.

Nutmeg Oil – Recommended for muscle aches.

Pine Oil – Stimulates blood flow and relaxes pain.

Almond Oil – Recommended for restoring skin tissue and skin nourishing.

Chamomile Oil – Recommended for treating acne, wounds, and cuts.

Jojoba Oil – Moisturizes and nourishes the skin, hair, and fingernails.

Coconut Oil – Anti-bacterial and treats inflammation. Moisturizes the skin and the hair. Removes makeup naturally.

MELT AND POUR DYING SOAP

SUPPLIES

Raw Soap Flakes
Soap Coloring
Oils, Spices and Herbs
Heat Resistant Glass Utensil
Fire / Microwave
Mixing Tool
Silicon Mold / Heat Resistant Container
Alcohol Spray

PROJECT

Place the soap flakes in the glass utensil and melt them. If you are using a double boiler turn off the fire before the soap completely liquefies. Mix slowly to keep the soap's temperature and texture. Once the flakes have melted, add a bit of color and gently mix. If it's a powdered color, dissolve a small amount in water and then add it to the soap.

Starting with a small amount of color allows you to control the shade. Once the color meets your approval, add the oils, scent, herbs and spices. Mix it well and pour the soap into the mold. For a polished look, spray alcohol on the soap while it's liquid to free air bubbles.

Soap takes from 12-24 hours to dry, depending on room temperature. If you don't have the patience, the process can be sped up by placing the soap in the freezer for 2-3 hours, depending on freezer strength. After the soap is completely dried, pull it gently from the mold.

LAYERED SOAP

SUPPLIES

Opaque Soap Flakes
Translucent Soap Flakes
Soap Coloring
Oils / Spices / Herbs
Heat-Resistant Glass Utensil
Pot / Microwave
Mixing Tool
Silicon Mold / Heat-Resistant Container
Alcohol Spray

PROJECT

Put the opaque soap flakes in a heat safe glass and melt them. If you are using a double boiler turn the fire off before the soap completely liquefies. Mix slowly to keep the soap's temperature and texture. Once the flakes have melted, add a bit of color and gently mix. If it's a powdered color, dissolve a small amount in water and then add it to the soap. Starting with a small amount of color allows you to control the shade. Once the color meets your

approval, add the oils, scent, herbs and spices. Mix it well and pour the first layer of translucent soap, and let it dry for at least 4-8 hours, depends on room temperature.
Start making the second layer following the same instructions, this time using the opaque soap. Once it melts, pour it on top of the translucent soap and wait for it to harden. For a polished look, spray alcohol on the soap when it's liquid to free air bubbles. Soap takes between 12-24 hours to dry, depending on room temperature. If you don't have the patience, the process can be sped up by placing the soap in the freezer for 2 to 3 hours, depending on freezer strength. After the soap is completely hard, pull it gently from the mold.

Add herbs, nutritious grains, leaves and seeds, to create textures in the soap to stimulate blood flow and infuse the exfoliating effect recommended for your skin.

CANDLE MAKING

Don't you just love the feeling when a candle is lit?
Everything feels more special and romantic.
In this chapter, I will show you the best technique to make candles at your own home using your favorite scents and colors.

Children under 14 must be accompanied by an adult. Do not leave the heating wax unattended. It is highly flammable

WAX MELTING METHODS

Double Boiler or Bain-Marie
A method borrowed from the world of fine cooking that uses two stacked pots to make a double boiler. For soap melting, we will use a pot and heat-resistant glass utensil. Do not use a plastic utensil or any unknown material. This method is used when direct fire will harm the quality of materials or burn them. Because wax is a very heat-sensitive material, it can easily decompose. Therefore, turn off the fire before the wax is completely liquefied. The boiling water will help the wax to fully melt.

Microwave
Melting wax in a microwave must be done using a heat-resistant glass utensil. Heat wax for 10 to 20 seconds, repeat as needed, according to microwave strength.

HOW TO MAKE A CANDLE

SUPPLIES

Wax Flakes
Candle Wicks
Heat Resistant Glass
Microwave / Pot
Heat Resistant Glass / Mold
Wax Coloring
Scents / Oils
Hot Glue Gun
Scissors
Pencil

PROJECT

Take a heat-resistant decorative jar and glue the wick to the bottom center using a hot glue gun. Set it aside. Place the wax flakes in the other glass container and melt them. If you are using a double boiler and not the microwave turn off the fire before the wax completely liquefied. Mix slowly to retain the wax temperature and texture. Mix the colors until you get the color you wish. Add the scent or oil to the wax mixture and stir. If you wish to create a natural mosquito and insect repellent, pour a generous amount of citronella oil into the candle wax while it is still liquefied. Pour the wax into the heat resistant jar or mold and hold the wick in up the center by attaching the top end of the wick to a long thin object. Wrap the wick around thin long tool and let it cool at room temperature for 4 to 5 hours. Once the wax hardens, cook the wick up to 2 cm from the wax. In order to extend the candles life, shorten the wick before lighting it. Shortening the wick will ensure good stable burning.

RECYCLING ART

COVERED BOTTLE

SUPPLIES
Glass Bottle
Rope / Hemp
Hot Glue Gun
Scissors

PROJECT
Place dots of glue on the bottle's bottom and wrap the rope around the bottle upwards. Repeat this step until the bottle is completely covered. Cut off any excess.

PRINGLES INTO VASE

SUPPLIES
Pringles Container
Stones / Ornaments
Paint
Paint brush
Hot Glue Glue

PROJECT
Empty the container and clean it. Paint it to give it a uniform coat and set to dry.
Glue stones or any ornaments on the container and set to dry.

TOILET PAPER ROLL ART

SUPPLIES

Toilet Paper Rolls
Scissors
Hot Glue Gun / White Glue

Toilet paper rolls are an ecological and inexpensive materials that can be found in every home.
They are great as supplies that can be transformed into a work of art.

PROJECT

Press on the rolls in flatten them. Cut them into three equal parts and glue each of them to each other. This is the base of your project. Add as many petals as you wish and create the shape you like. If you wish to glue the petals with regular glue, use clothespins to keep them in place.

The Craft Kingdom   Want more Projects? Visit us on Youtube   55.....

TOILET PAPER AS GIFT BOXES 1

SUPPLIES
Toilet Paper Rolls
Crepe Paper
Ribbons

PROJECT
Place a roll in the center of the crepe paper and insert the gift into the roll. Make sure the roll is centered from side to side on the crepe paper. Wrap the paper around the roll until it is fully covered. Cut away the remainder of the crepe paper on each end as if you were wrapping a candy. Tie a 20-15 cm ribbons to each end to decorate it.

TOILET PAPER AS A PRESENT BOX 2

SUPPLIES
Toilet Paper Rolls
Decorative Paper
Rope
Clear Tape

PROJECT
Place the roll on the paper and insert the gift into the roll. Wrap the paper around the roll and fold the ends of the paper into the roll, and use a tape to close it.
If you wish to decorate the present, tie 15-20 cm rope around it.

PLASTIC BOTTLE INTO BRACELET

SUPPLIES

Plastic Bottle
Marker
X-Acto Knife
Clear Tape
Fabric
Hot Glue Gun

PROJECT

Draw two lines around the bottle approximately 4 to 5 cm apart or to the width you want for your bracelet. Cut along your lines forming a ring. Make one cut through the ring so that it is open. Fit it to your arm to determine what size will fit you correctly. Use your glue gun to reattach the two ends to create a ring in the size you need. Wrap the plastic with tape to seal the edges and to set the bracelet size. Wrap the bracelet with the fabric until you cover the whole bracelet. Glue the fabric using a hot glue gun.

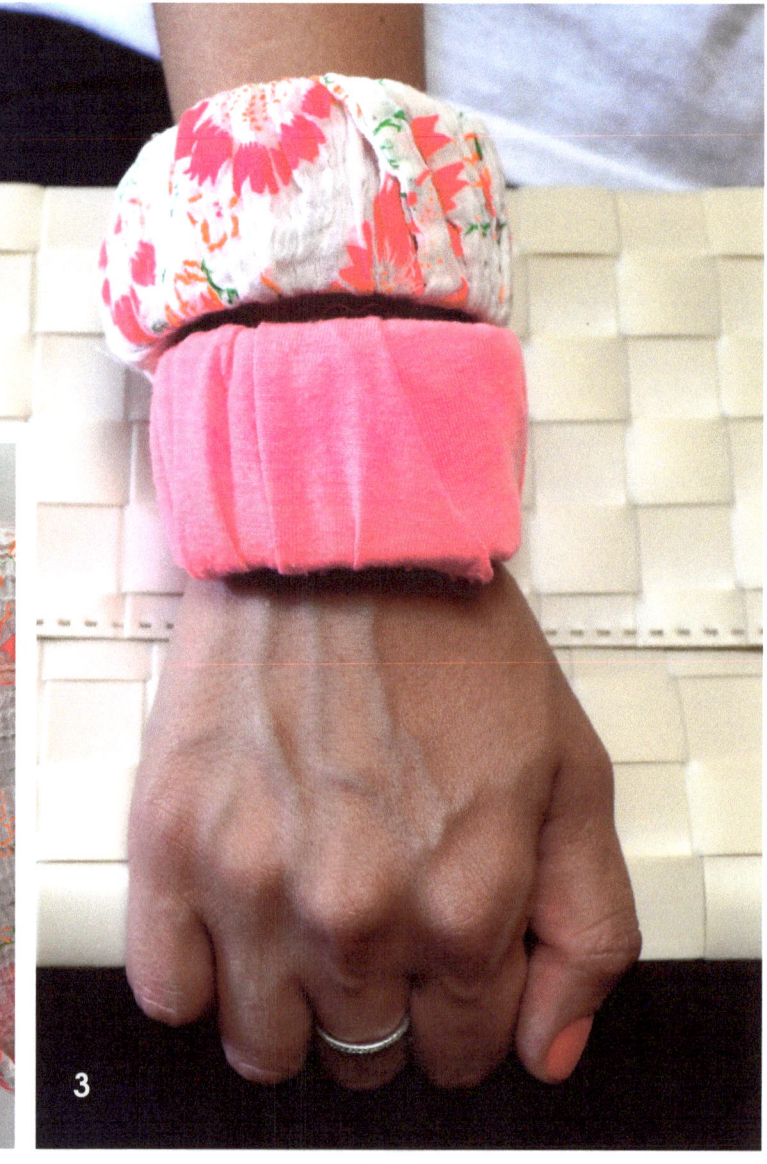

PISTACHIOS SHELLS INTO ORNAMENTS

SUPPLIES

Hot Glue Gun
Cardboard / Heavy Paper
Pistachio Shells

PROJECT

Clean the pistachio shells. Glue the first shell to the center of the cardboard or paper. Glue the second shell inside the first. Continue gluing the remaining shells underneath the first two shells. Arrange them in any design you wish. For a polished look, you can paint the shells in any color you like.

REPURPOSING

If you look around your home, you will be surprised to see that you are surrounded by objects that you don't really use. However, they can be turned into new objects as well as works of art. Break the rules and give a new meaning to things around you using your ideas and creativity. Remember, before you throw something away or let it sit accumulating dust, see if it can be used in an original and exciting way.

GLASSES INTO AN ORGANIZER

SUPPLIES
6 Glasses / Jars
Hot Glue Gun

PROJECT
Glue three glasses to each other making a triangular base. Glue two additional glasses to the base. Finally, glue the last glass to the top of the pyramid and set it aside to dry.
This stand can be built in different sizes - the more glasses or jars you use, the bigger it becomes.

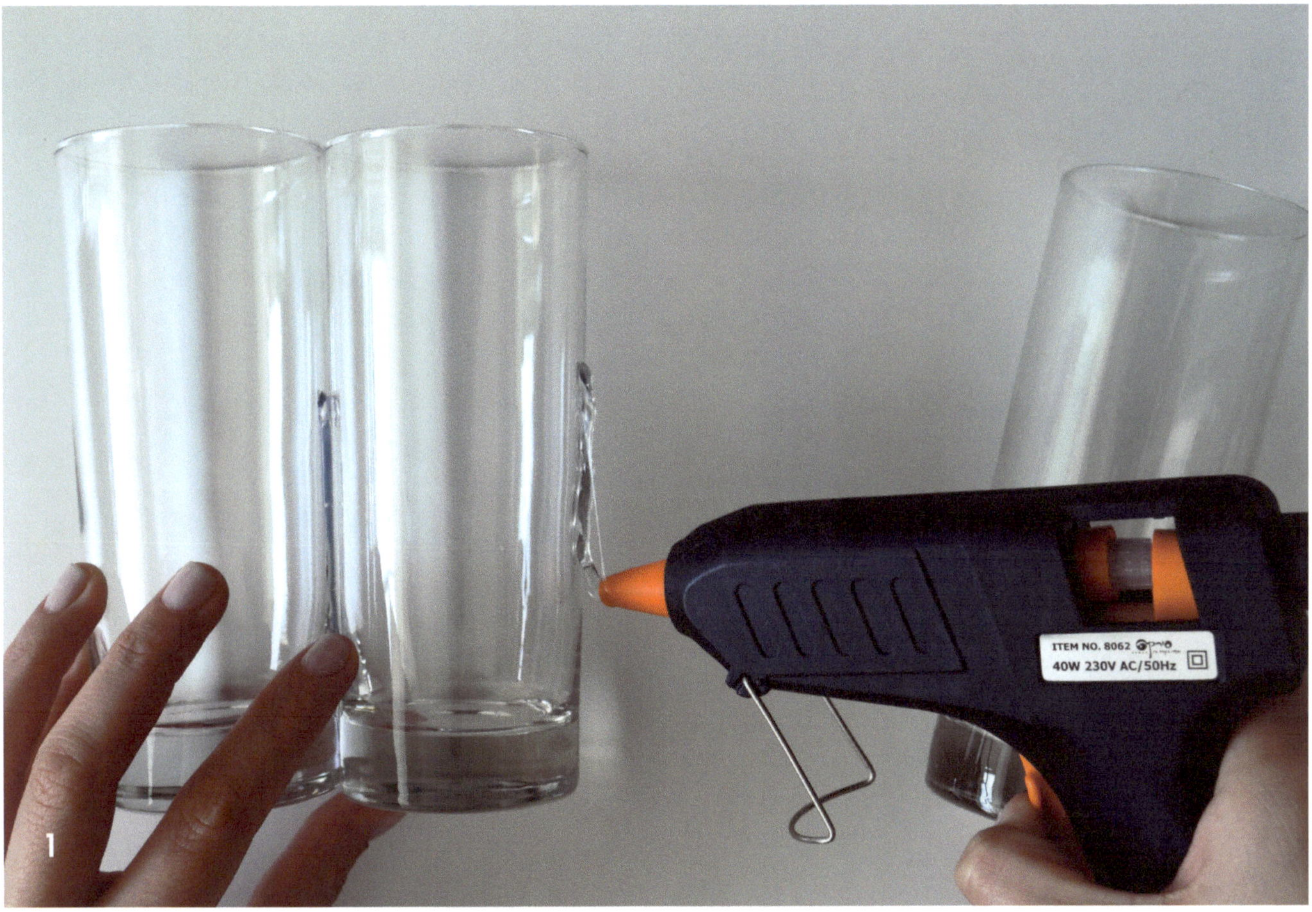

PLACEMAT CLUTCH

SUPPLIES

Placemat
Hot Glue Gun
5-10 cm Velcro Tape
Buttons

PROJECT

Fold the placemat into three sections. Two of the sections should be the same width. They will form the body of your clutch. The third section will be narrower and will form the flap which will close the clutch. Press firmly. Mark the inside edges of the two sections which form the body of the clutch. Glue the sides of the body along the edges that you marked. If needed, use clips to secure the clutch after applying the hot glue. Glue the Velcro tape onto the inside of the body of the clutch and the flap. It will become the closure as shown in pictures 6 ,5, and 7. Use your hot glue gun to attach the buttons as shown in pictures 7-6. Set it aside to dry. If you wish to decorate the clutch you can use your buttons or a decoration of your choice.

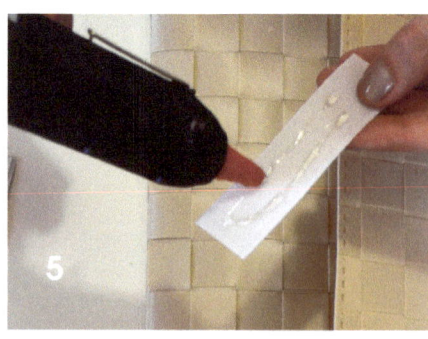

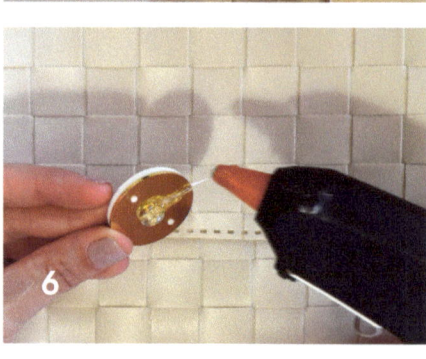

SOCK HOLDER

SUPPLIES
Glass / Mug
Sock
Scissors

PROJECT
Trim the ankle part of the socks.
Dress and adjust the sock on the glass.
If you are using a mug, cut a tiny circle on the side of the sock, dress the sock on the mug and stretch the hole to fit the mug handle.

SWEATER PILLOW COVERS

SUPPLIES

Sweaters / T-shirts
Scissors
Sewing Tools / Fabric Glue
Pillow Stuffing

PROJECT

Select a sweater or T-shirt and place the pillow form inside of it. Make sure it fits properly. Remove the pillow form. Cut the neck, chest and sleeves off to create a square. Turn the sweater inside out. Sew or glue the cover edges together leaving one side open. Reinsert the pillow form. Close the final side.

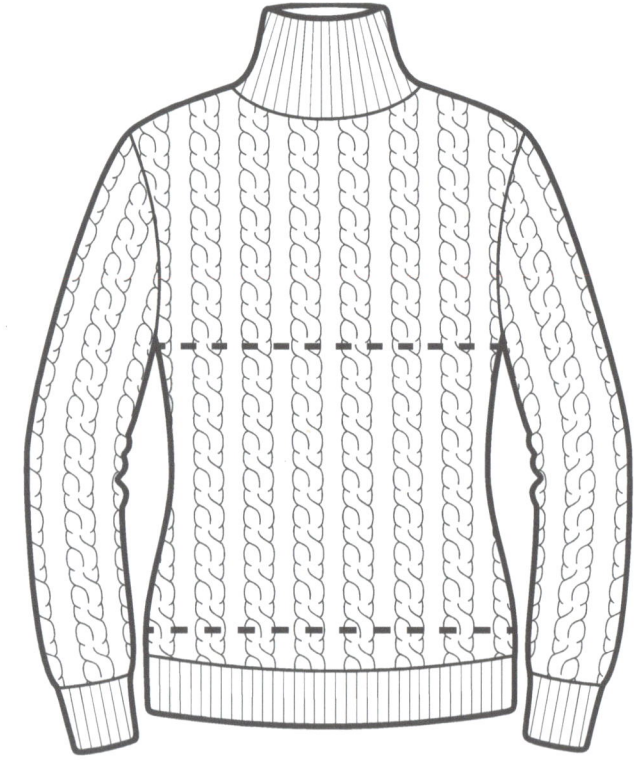

PICTURE INTO INSPIRATION BOARD

SUPPLIES
Frame with Glass
Magnetic Paint
Paintbrush
Inspiration Items
Scissors
Magnets Sheets
Glue

PROJECT
Clean the picture of all dust and dirt. Paint the picture glass with the magnetic paint. Follow the instructions on the paint container. Once the glass has been coated evenly and the paint is dry check to make sure the magnets stick on the glass. If not, add extra layers of magnetic paint until it sticks. Cut out your inspiration items, glue them to the magnets, and set them out to dry. Place them on the board.

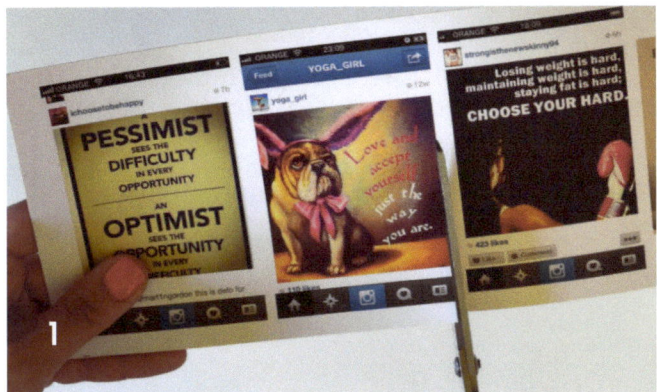

1

2

PILLOW CASE INTO A BAG

SUPPLIES

Pillowcase
Pen / Marker
Scissors
Sewing Tool / Fabric Glue

PROJECT

Find the pillow case pocket and sew or glue it. If you are working with a pillowcase that closes with a zipper, you don't need to sew or glue the pocket. Fold the pillow in half and create a vertical rectangle. Mark a quarter circle on the left unfolded side of the pillowcase (pic 3) and trim it using the mark as a guide. Open the fold and reveal the bag.

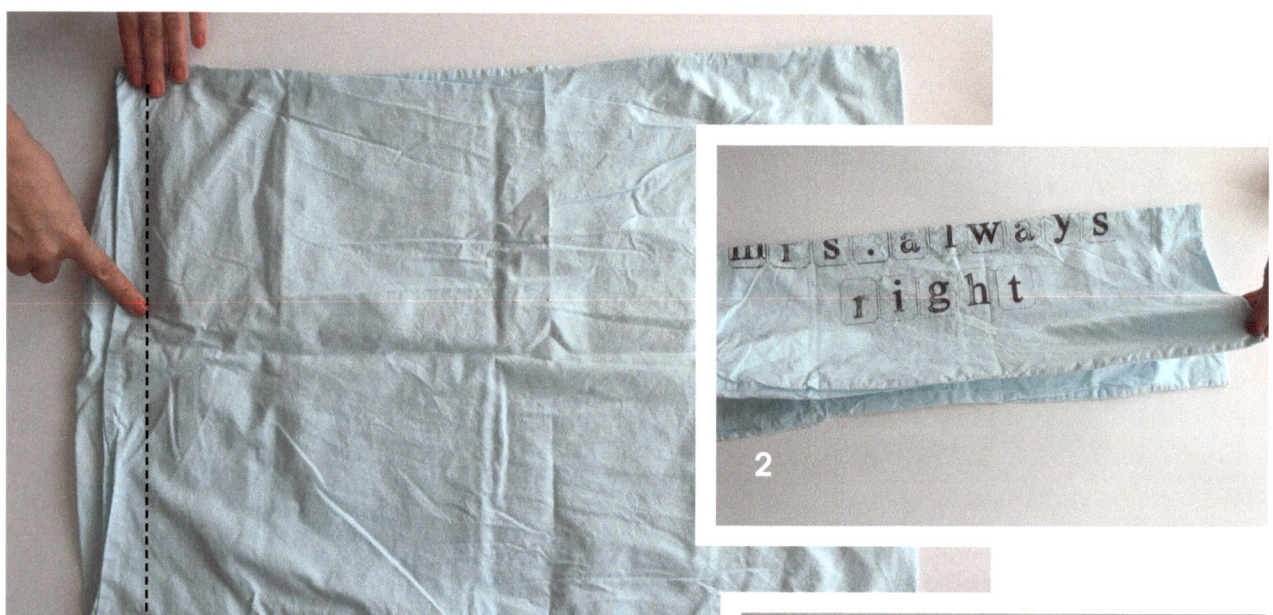

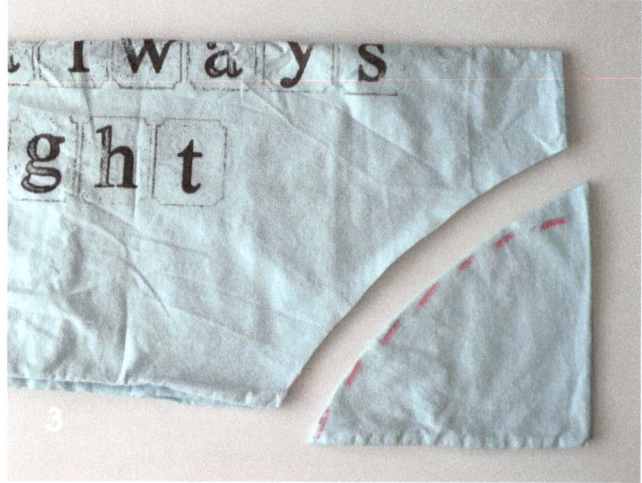

ACCESSORIES

ROPE NECKLACE

SUPPLIES
Rope
Metal Tube
Magnetic Clasp
Glue
Scissors

PROJECT
Cut the rope to the desired length using the necklace diagram below. Thread the tube to the center of the rope. Squeeze glue into the two magnetic clasps. Insert the end of the rope into the magnetic clasp ends. Set it out to dry.

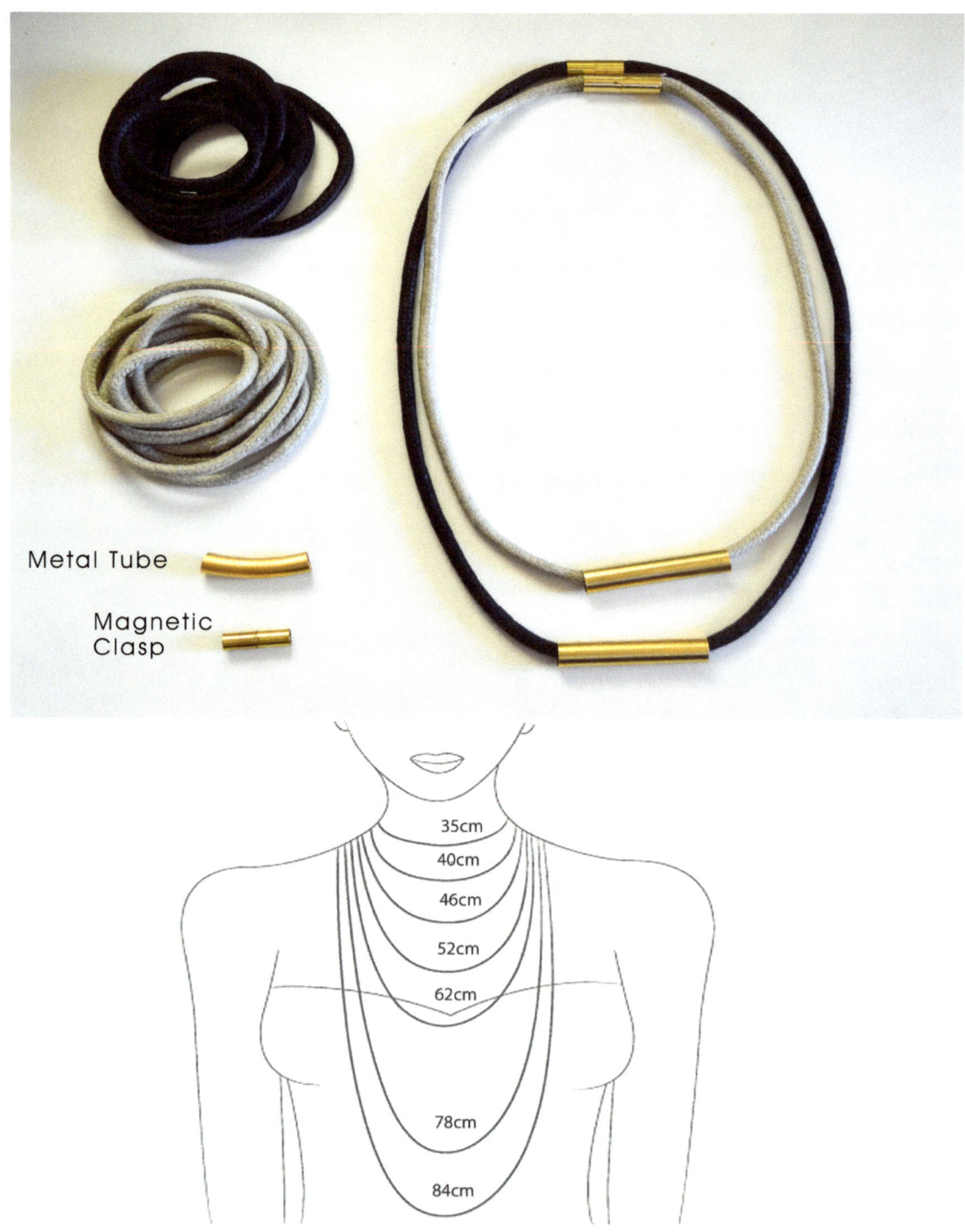

PENDANT NECKLACE

SUPPLIES
Closed Chain
Pendant
Jump Ring
2 Pliers

PROJECT
Open the jump ring using the pliers. Attach the pendant to the chain using the jump ring. Make sure the ends of the jump ring are securely closed and that the pendant is securely on the chain.

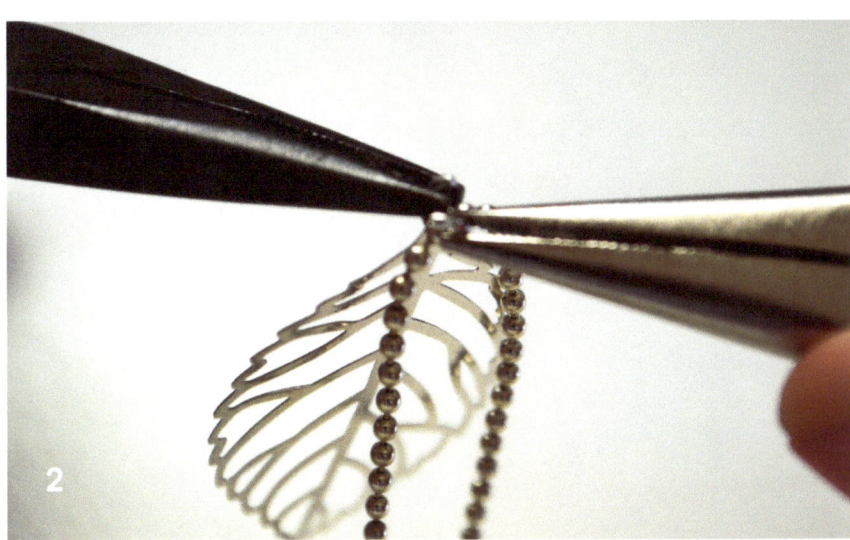

The Craft Kingdom — Want more Projects? Visit us on Youtube

PEARLED BOBBY PIN

SUPPLIES

Bobby Pins
Thin Wire
Pearls / Beads
Scissors

PROJECT

Cut between 5-7cm wire and thread the pearl to the wire, placing it in its center (pic 1). Bend the two ends of the wire (pic 2) and start twisting the wires around each other (pic 3). Insert the wire inside the bobby pin curve and wrap around the bobby pin until the pearl is securely holds onto it.

HAIR EMBELLISHMENTS

SUPPLIES

15-20 cm Chain
2 Jump Rings
2 Pliers
2 Bobby Pins

PROJECT

Use the length of chain that gives you the look you want. Trim off any excess. Insert the jump rings on each end of the chain using the pliers. Thread the bobby pins onto the jump rings and place the embellishment at the back of the head making a smile shape.

The Craft Kingdom — Want more Projects? Visit us on Youtube

PAPER FLOWER EMBELLISHMENTS

SUPPLIES

Bobby Pins
Paper / Fabric Flowers with Wire Stem

PROJECT

Thread the flower stem through the bobby pin and start wrapping it around the pin curve until the flower is securely on the pin.

FLOWERY HEADBAND

SUPPLIES
Paper / Fabric Flowers with Iron Stem
Plastic Headband

PROJECT
Place a flower in the center of the headband and start wrapping the wire stem around it until the flower is secured. Repeat this step making sure that all of the flowers face the same direction. Continue until the headband is completely covered with flowers.

JEWELRY RACK

SUPPLIES

Wooden Board
Drawer Pulls
Hot Glue Gun
Foam Mounting Squares

PROJECT

Space the pulls evenly along the board. Glue the handles onto the board and set it aside to dry. Once it has dried glue the foam mounting squares onto the back. Hang it on your wall or inside the closet.

DECORATED KEYCHAIN

SUPPLIES

Keychain
Twine
10 Bolts
Scissors

PROJECT

Cut the twine into three lengths of 20-25 cm. Gather them together and tie them around the keychain using a lark's head knot. Start braiding the twine. After a few centimeters start threading the bolts onto the braid each time from a different side. Tie the braid. Trim the excess and add your keys.

HOW TO MAKE A PAPILLON BROOCH

SUPPLIES

2 13-15 cm Wide Ribbons
2 6-8 cm Narrow Ribbons
Scissors
Hot Glue Gun
Hair Clip
Measuring Tape

PROJECT

Cut two equals strips of the wide ribbon about 13-15 cm long. Fold the ribbons in half until there is a visible crease. Place glue on the crease and fold the two ends to the center. Set aside to dry. Pinch the ribbon using your fingers as shown in picture 3. Repeat this step with the second strip of the wide ribbon. Glue the two bows to each other and set aside to dry. Cut 2 6-8cm lengths of the narrow ribbon. Using one of the ribbons along the top of the hair clip to cover it. Set it aside to dry. Wrap the second ribbon around both the hair clip and the bow. Glue the ribbon to the back of the hair clip to secure the bow. Cut away the excess ribbon.

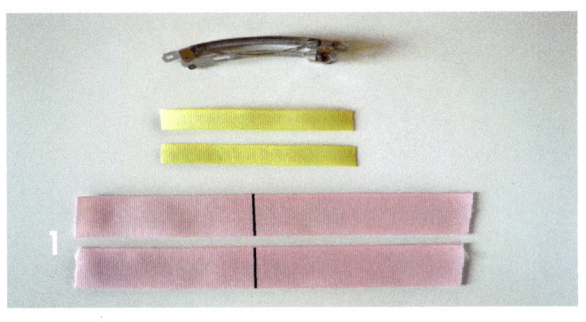
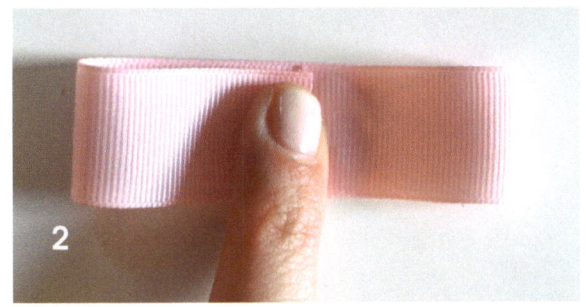

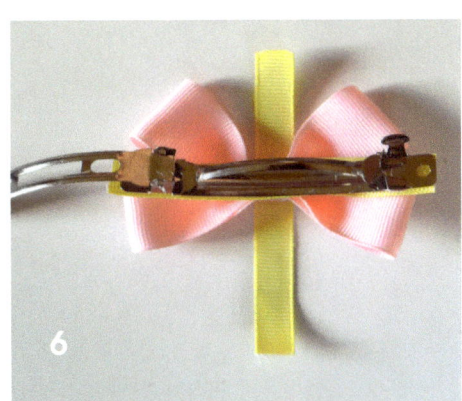
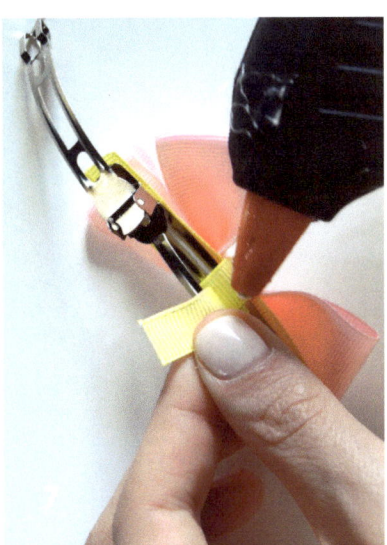

The Craft Kingdom — Want more Projects? Visit us on Youtube

JEWELRY ORGANIZERS

SUPPLIES

Rubber Play Animal
Longer Screws
Plate
Paint
Glue

PROJECT

Attach the screw in the center of the rubber animals until they are secure. Paint them and set them aside to dry. Place the animals in the center of the plate and glue them into place. After they dry organize your jewelry.

PET NECKLACE

SUPPLIES

Elastic Thread
Beads
Scissors
Measuring Tape

PROJECT

Measure your pet's neck using a piece of the unstretched elastic thread and add an extra 5 to 7 cm to that length. Cut the elastic and tie it at one end so that the beads will not fall off. Leave a small tail of elastic. Thread your beads being careful not to stretch the elastic or your necklace may not fit. Tie the ends of the necklace together. Make sure the necklace can easily go over your pet's head.

FABRICS AND TEXTILES

Before you spend your money buying fabric, take a peek in your closet. You may find unused clothing and other items that you can use. They can provide you with exciting prints, colors, and textures.

PET SCARF

SUPPLIES
Fabric
Mesuring Tape
Scissors
Fabric Pen

PROJECT
Measure your pet's neck circumference and add an extra 4-5 cm to the lengh. Mark it on the fabric along with two lines using the same lengh, to create an equilateral triangular as shown in the sketch above. Cut the fabric as marked and tie the scarf around your pet's neck. If you want to make a scarf for yourself, follow the same process, this time using your neck circumference.

NOTEBOOKS COVER

SUPPLIES

Notebook
Fabric
Scissors
Glue
Button

PROJECT

Lay your fabric down. Place the notebook in the center of the fabric and make sure that the fabric is bigger than the notebook when it is open. Cut your fabric to allow a 5-3 cm seam allowance on the bottom and top of the notebook. Wrap the fabric around the notebook and trim it. Glue the fabric to the notebook. Cut a tiny square (pic 3) in order for the notbook to open and close easily. If you wish to decorate, glue a button on the notebook cover.

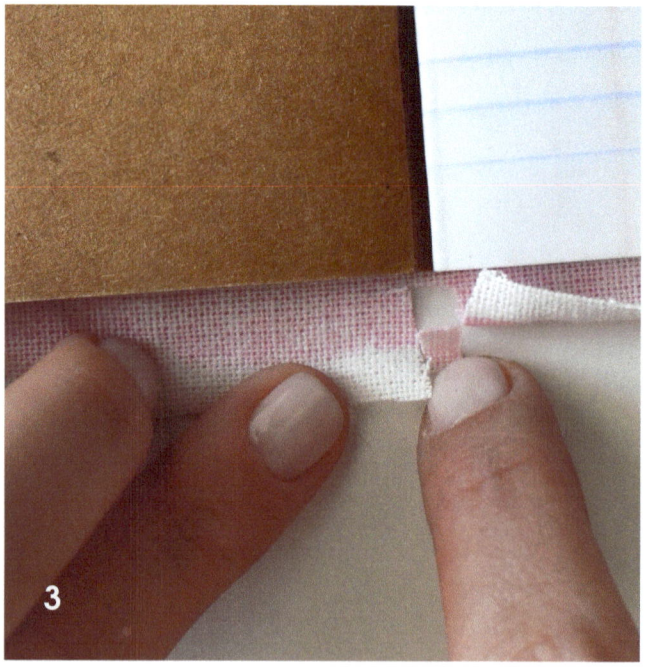

GIFT WRAPPING USING A DOILY

SUPPLIES

Doily / Fabric
Wrapping Paper
Perforated
Scissors
Ribbon

PROJECT

Punch a hole in the wrapping paper using the perforated (pic 1). Cut the doily in the center making two triangles (pic 2). Attach the cut doily to the wrapping paper and thread the ribbon to them both. Tie the ribbon to close the present.

FABRIC JAR TOPPERS

SUPPLIES

Fabric
Jar
Strine / Twine
Scissors
Fabric Pen

PROJECT

Place the jar lid on the fabric and use it to trace a template. Cut the fabric so that it is 2 to 3 cm larger than the lid. Replace the jar lid. Place the cut fabric over the jar using the string or twine.

PATCHWORK DECORATIONS

SUPPLIES

Heart Template (Page 106)
Fabric
Scissors
Lace
Glue / Sewing Tools

PROJECT

Cut out the heart template from page 106. Trace it on the fabric and cut out the shape. Trim the lace to fit across the heart and glue it on. You can can glue or sew the patch onto anything you wish to decorate.

NEEDLEWORK PATTERN INSPIRATION

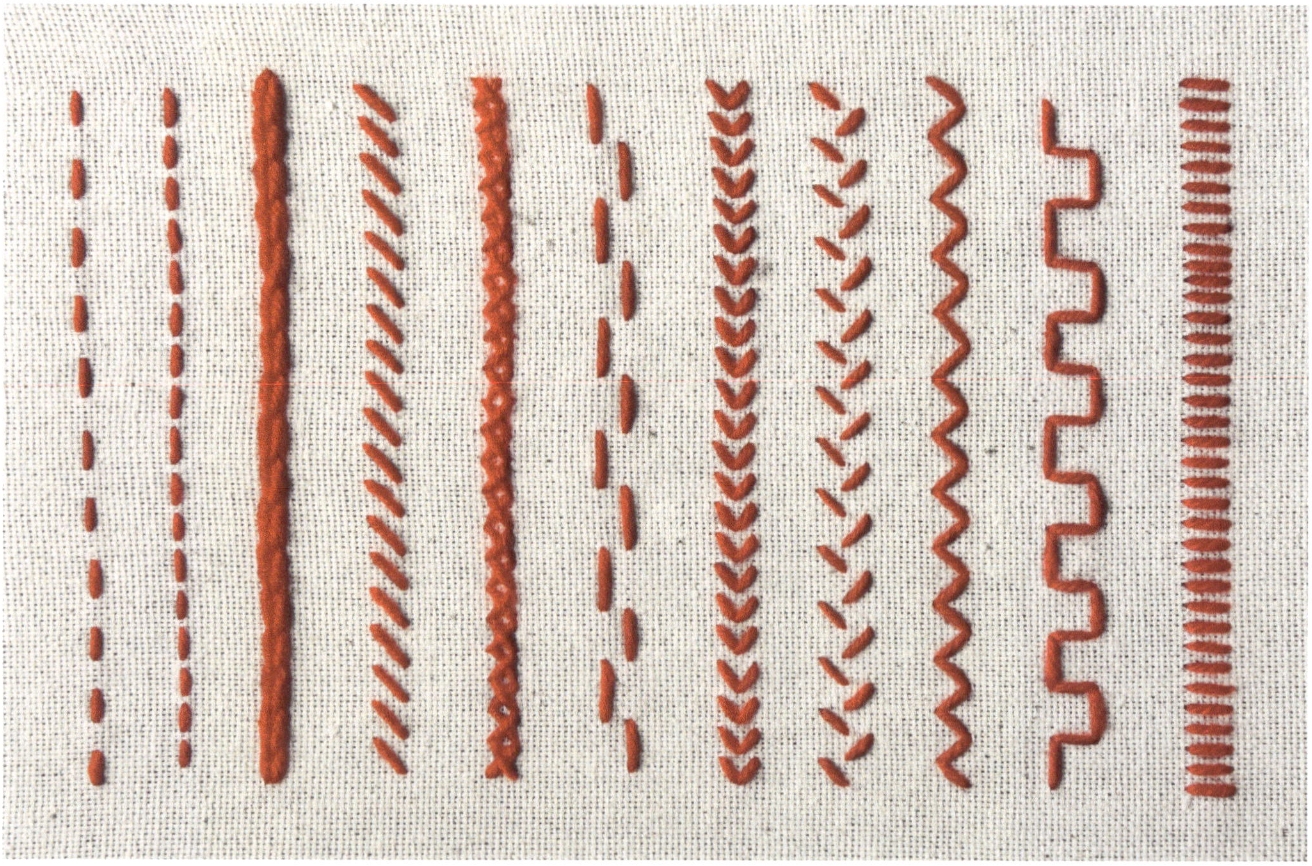

FABRIC CHRISTMAS ORNAMENTS

SUPPLIES

Christmas Tree Template (Page 106)
Fabric
Fabric Pen
Niddle and Thread
Buttons
Pillow Stuffing
Scissors

PROJECT

Cut out the template from page 106. Place it on the fabric and trace it. Cut two pieces. Sew them together leaving a small hole to insert the pillow stuffing. Stuff it. Sew up the small hole. Decorate the tree by sewing buttons on it to look like Christmas balls.

FABRIC HEART DECORATION

SUPPLIES

Heart Template (Page 106)
Fabrics
Pen
Pillow stuffing
Sewing Tools / Fabric Glue
Buttons and Ribbons
Thread
Scissord

PROJECT

Cut the heart template (Page 106), place it on the fabric, mark it and cut it. Repete this step this time cut one half of the heart using one fabric and the second half using a different fabric, leave a seam allowance. Glue or sew the halfed hearts to each other, and glue or sew the two hearts together, leaveing a small hole. Insert the pillow stuffing and insert the thread. Glue or sew the hole in place. For extra decoration, you can add buttons and ribbons to the heart.

QUILT

SUPPLIES

Square Template (Page 110)
Fabrics
Fabric Pen
Scissors
Sewing Tools

PROJECT

Choose the size of the blanket you wish to make and cut as many squares as you need according to the size you chose. Cut the template from page 110, place it on the fabric and cut the fabric matching the template. In order to make a regular blanket size, you will need to cut 200 fabric squares - 10 squares for the width and 20 squares for the length. After cutting the squares, place them in your desired order and start sewing them to each other, while they are on their faded side, using the seam allowance on the template as youe sewing guide. Cut another fabric to match the squares blanket and sew them to each other using their opposite side. Leave a small hole around 5 cm, flip the blanket back to it's correct side and sew the remaining hole.

BUTTONS

BUTTONS FOR DECORATION

Choose your favorite buttons and decorate your clothes, accessories and fabrics

The Craft Kingdom

BUTTONS BRACELET

SUPPLIES

String
Buttons
Scissors
Measuring Tape

PROJECT

Cut two equal length of string about 8-10 cm long and thread them through the buttonholes using loop knots as shown. Wrap the bracelet around the wrist, tie it and cut away any excess thread.

BUTTONS HAIR CLIP

SUPPLIES

Hair Clip
Buttons
Ribbon
Hot Glue Gun

PROJECT

Cut a length of the ribbon long enough to cover the clip. Glue the ribbon along the top of the hair clip. Cut off any excess. Set it aside to dry. Select your favorite buttons and arrange them along the top of the clip in a design you like. Glue them to the clip and set it aside to dry.

BUTTON LETTERS

SUPPLIES

Letter Template (Page 108)
Buttons
Sewing Tools
Fabric

PROJECT

Cut out the template and trace around it onto the fabric. Cut it out. Place the paper template on the fabric that you cut out. Place the buttons on the template and arrange them as you wish. Sew each button through the paper and the fabric. Repeat until the letter is fully covered. Rip away the paper template from the fabric. If you wish to do any other letter you can search online for more templates and print them.

USING BUTTONS TO WRAP GIFT

SUPPLIES

Wrapped Gift
2 Buttons
Twine / String
Scissors

PROJECT

Cut four pieces of string to the right size to wrap your gift. Thread the strings through the buttonholes of the two buttons using a loop knot. Wrap the two strings around the gift with one going across and the other wrapping around the box top to bottom. Make sure your buttons are placed nicely in the center front of your gift. Tie them off on the back of the gift cutting off away any excess.

PAPER

PAPER EMBELLISHMENT

Cut letters or other shapes from a pretty piece of paper with a design and color you like. You can use it to decorate greeting cards, books, or any other items that you wish to embellish.

PAPER GREETING CARDS

Cut music notes paper and burn the edges. Decorate it using fabric flowers.

PAPER PUNCH EMBELLISHMENTS

SUPPLIES

Papers
Paper Punch
White Glue
Surface to Decorate

PROJECT

Punch shapes out of your paper and lay them out. Arrange them on the paper or other surface you wish to decorate. Glue them and set them aside to dry.

PLACE CARDS

SUPPLIES
Sturdy Rectangular Paper
Pencil
Colored Pencils
X-Acto Knife

PROJECT
Set your paper down in front of you in the landscape position. Fold the top of the paper down until it meets the bottom edge. Crease it. Draw a sketch of the object you choose in the center of your card. Cut out the top half of your picture, but only the portion above the crease. Separate the object carefully. Fold the paper in half so that he can stand on it.

GLITTER PAPER DECORATION

SUPPLIES

Decorative Paper Punch
2 sheets of Papers
White Glue
Soft Brush
Glitter

PROJECT

Take your first sheet of paper and punch out your shape. Place the punched paper on top of the second sheet. This will be your template. Spread glue inside of the hole only. Spread the glitter on the glue. Remove your template carefully and set the card aside to dry. After it has dried thoroughly turn the page upside down and shake away any loose glitter.

HOW TO MAKE A TAG

SUPPLIES

Tag Template (Page 112)
Cardboard
Pen
Rope / Twine
Scissors

PROJECT

Cut the template (Page 112), place it on the cardboard and mark the cardboard. Cut the cardboard, punch a hole in the top center of the tag and insert the rope in a loop knot and attach to your gift.

HOW TO MAKE A GIFT BOX

SUPPLIES

Gift Box Template (Page 112)
Printed Cardboard
Rope / Twine
Pen
Scissors

PROJECT

Cut the template (Page 112), place it on the cardboard and mark the cardboard. Cut the cardboard and punch four holes in each corner. Bend the cardboard inwards and thread the rope through all holes. Place the gift inside the box and tie it.

PAPER NAPKINS

In the past, napkins were just napkins - a wonderful, colorful addition to a set table as well as a great way to clean up messes. In addition, paper napkins are an amazing and inexpensive raw material for decorating items such as plates, glass containers, candlesticks, jars, candles, keys, and practically anything you wish.

NAPKIN DECORATION ON A GLASS

SUPPLIES
Plate
Decorative
Paper Napkin
Napkin Glue
Paintbrush
Scissors

PROJECT
Most decorative napkins are made of 2 to 3 layers. Separate your napkin between the layers. It is a bit like separating two sheets of toilet paper, so be patient. Cut out the object that you wish to use from the decorative layer. Brush a layer of glue on the plate where you wish. Carefully apply a thin layer of glue on top of the object using your paintbrush. Apply the object smoothly to the glued area. Set it aside to dry.

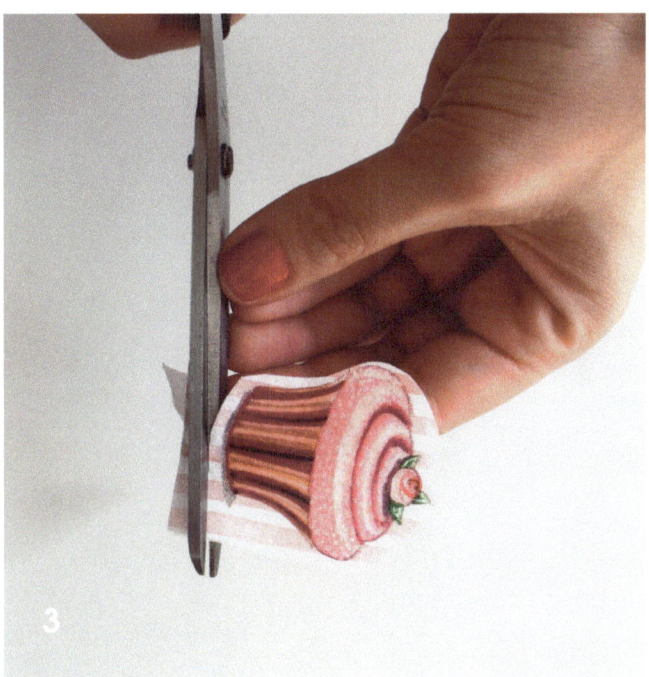

NAPKINS DECORATIONS ON CANDLES

SUPPLIES

Candle
Decorative Paper Napkin
White Glue
Paintbrush
Scissors

PROJECT

Wrap the decorative layer napkin around the candle that you choose to decorate overlapping just a bit. Cut away any excess. Apply a thin layer of glue on the candle. Wrap the napkin around the candle. Set it aside to dry. Attention: This candle is for decorative purposes only and is not meant to be lit.

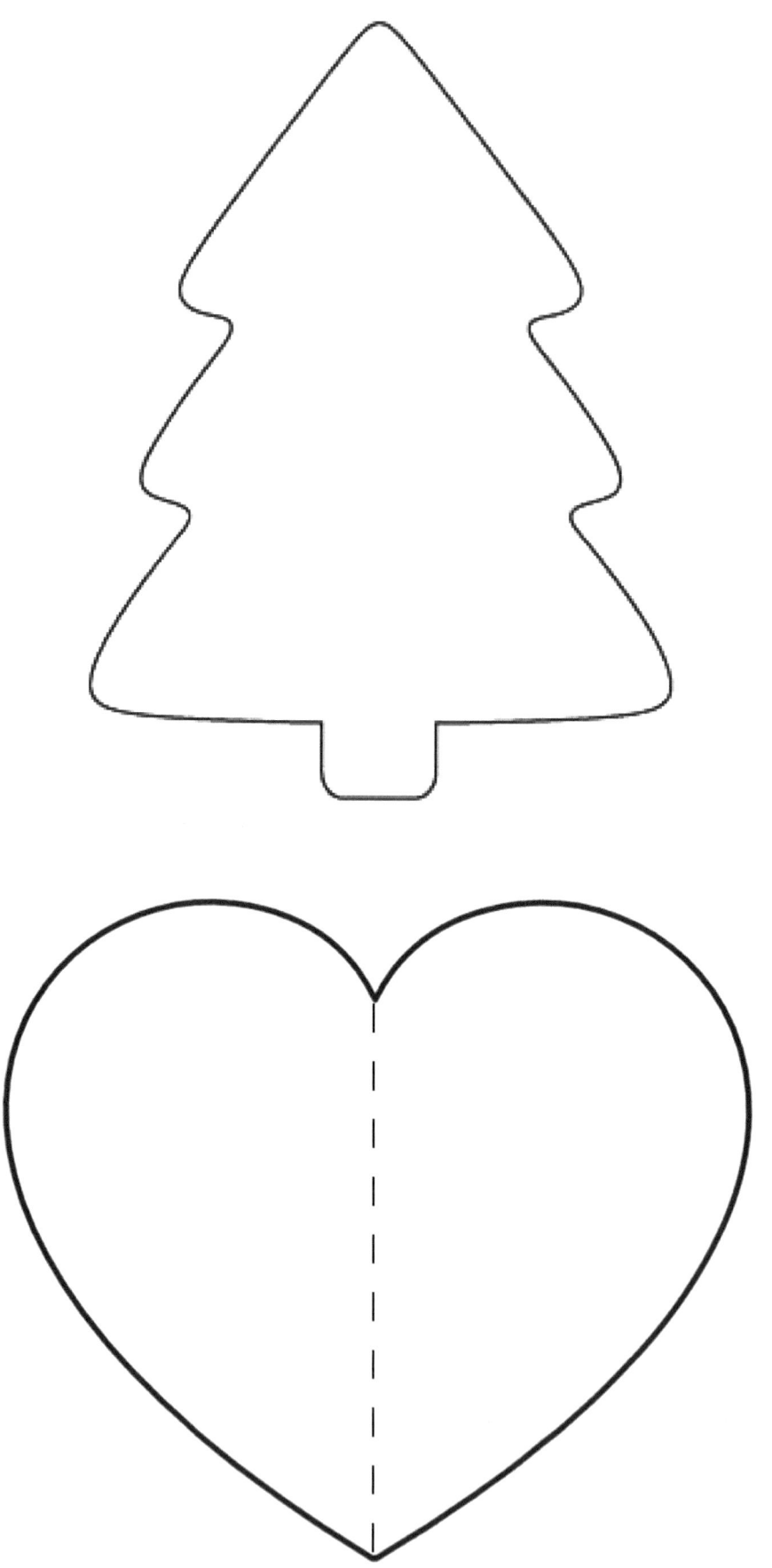

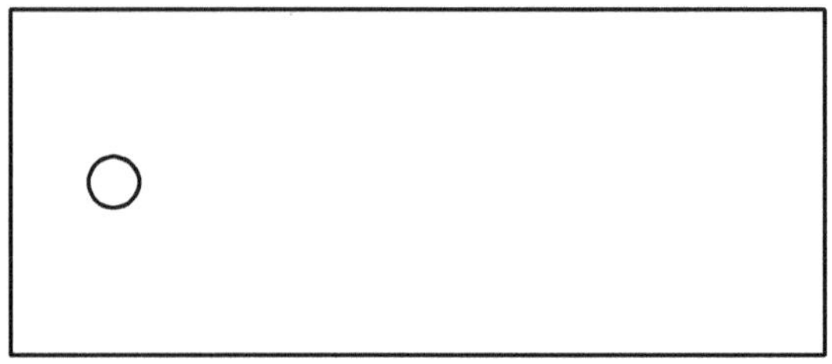

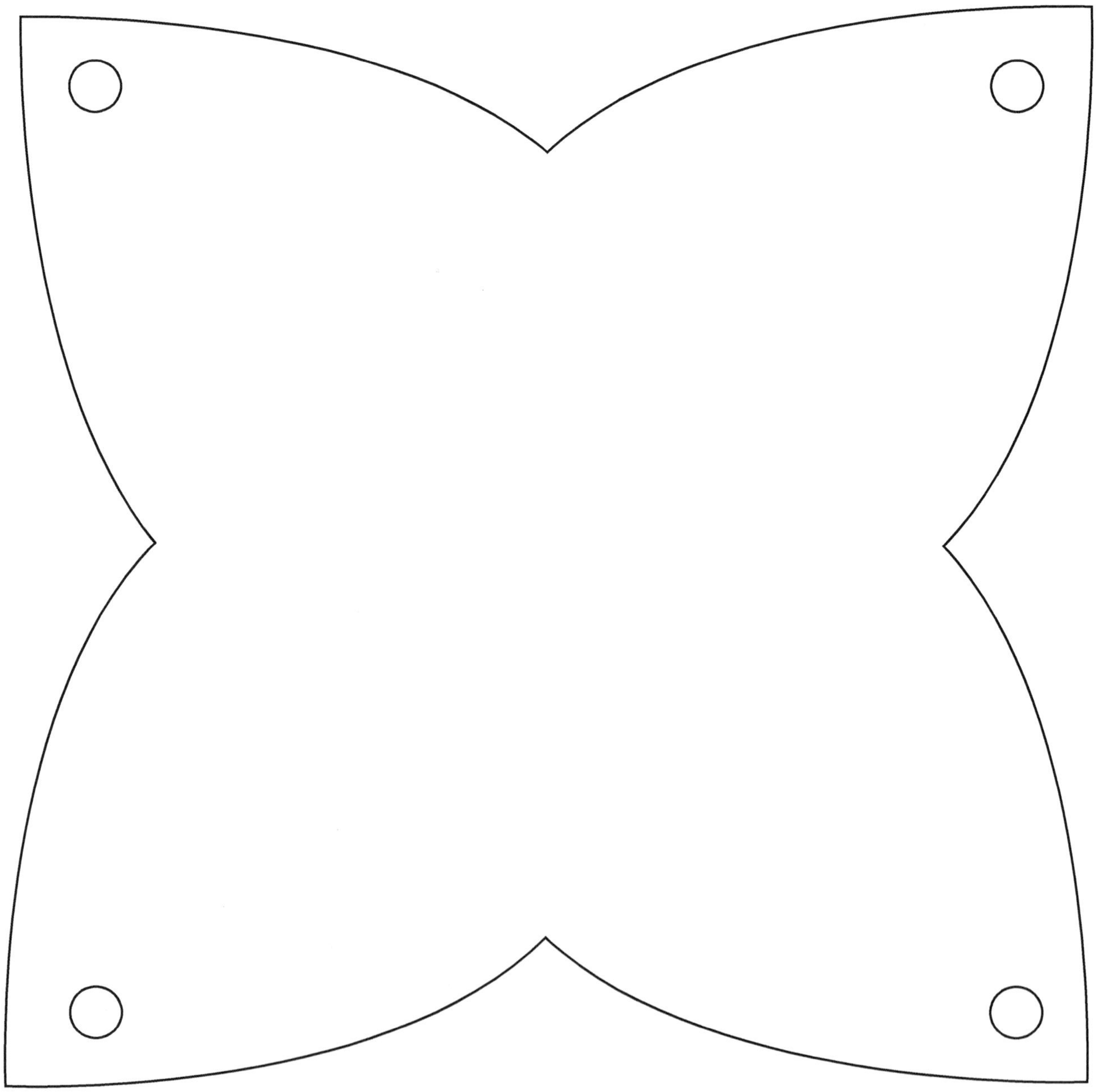

.....112

The Craft Kingdom

www.ingramcontent.com/pod-product-compliance
Lightning Source LLC
Chambersburg PA
CBHW041527220426
43670CB00003B/53